Marie Curie

Edwina Conner

Illustrations by Richard Hook

The Bookwright Press
New York · 1987

Great Lives

Beethoven
Louis Braille
Captain Cook
Marie Curie
Einstein
Elizabeth I
Elizabeth II
Anne Frank
Gandhi
Helen Keller

John F. Kennedy
Martin Luther King, Jr.
John Lennon
Ferdinand Magellan
Karl Marx
Napoleon
Florence Nightingale
Elvis Presley
William Shakespeare
Mother Teresa

First published in
the United States in 1987 by
The Bookwright Press
387 Park Avenue South
New York, NY 10016

First published in 1987 by
Wayland (Publishers) Limited
61 Western Road, Hove
East Sussex BN3 1JD, England

ISBN 0–531–18134–0

Library of Congress Catalog Card Number: 86–72822
Phototypeset by Kalligraphics Limited, Redhill, Surrey, England
Printed in Italy by G. Canale & C.S.p.A., Turin

Contents

A famous scientist

Cancer is a terrible disease, but we now know that many forms can be cured with different kinds of treatment. One important way to treat cancer is with radiotherapy. One night in 1898, after years of work in very difficult conditions, Marie Curie discovered radium, the element used in radiotherapy which helps to cure cancer. If it hadn't been for this discovery by Marie and Pierre Curie, radiotherapy would not exist.

Marie Curie became a very famous scientist, and her discovery caused excitement all over the world, yet she was quite uninterested in making any money for herself. She dedicated her life to science and to saving people's lives.

There was much sadness in her life, and she became ill through the effects of working with radioactive elements, but her determination and hard work won her a place among the most important scientists who have ever lived.

Early days

When the school inspector came to check that the children were being taught as the Russians had ordered, young Maria was often called on to answer questions.

Maria Sklodowska was born in Warsaw, Poland, on November 7, 1867. She had an older brother, Jozef, and three older sisters: Sofia, Bronya and Helena.

This was a very difficult time for Poles, because the country was ruled by the Russians. The people were supposed to speak Russian rather than Polish, and Poles with important jobs were forced out of work and replaced by Russians. When Maria was six, her father was made to give up his job. From then on the family had little money.

Maria was a small, timid child, but she was a good student. She had even taught herself to read before she went to school.

All school subjects had to be taught in Russian and the children learned only Russian history. But the Poles could not be stopped from teaching Polish to the children secretly. If they had been caught they would have been put in prison and punished.

Tiring times

While Maria was still very young, her sister Sofia and her mother became very ill and died of a lung disease called tuberculosis. The other children were looked after by housekeepers until Bronya left school and cared for them. It was a sad time for the Sklodowskas.

When she was fifteen, Maria won a gold medal at school for her studies, but her hard work had exhausted her. She was frail and tired. Her father said she must leave the city and spend a year with some relatives who lived on a farm in the south of Poland. She did, and for the first time in her life she forgot her studies and enjoyed dancing, sleigh rides and games in the snow.

She returned to Warsaw less thin, more relaxed and eager to work. But what could she do to earn her living?

Maria grew up in Warsaw, the capital city of Poland.

At home, Maria and her sisters all loved to read.

Two sisters

Maria's older sister Bronya decided that she wanted to become a doctor. It was impossible for women to go on to higher education in Warsaw. The university would not admit them. Her only chance was to get herself to the Sorbonne University in Paris. For this she needed money, and her father was not well off.

So Maria and Bronya worked out a plan. Bronya would go to Paris to study and Maria would take a job as a governess in the country and send the money she earned to Bronya. Later, Bronya would help Maria with her own education.

Maria hated her first job. She did not get on with the family at all. But the second family, the Zorawskis, who lived in the country village of Szczuki, were quite different. She became friends with the oldest daughter, Bronka, and enjoyed teaching her and the youngest child Andzia. While she was there, working seven hours a day with the Zorawski girls, she set up a school for the peasant children in the area teaching them Polish.

Farewell Poland

Soon Maria was teaching a class of eighteen children in her own room two extra hours a day — more on her days off.

At the same time, she became passionately interested in science, particularly physics and mathematics. She read books on these subjects and pored over them late at night and in the early morning, before work.

Bronya had managed to get to Paris, and now Maria wanted to go too. She must learn more. It was time to leave the Zorawskis. There was another reason why she had to get away. She had fallen in love with the son of the house, a good-looking young man with fair hair and a fine moustache called Kazimierz. It seems that he loved her too. But at this time she was merely a governess, and not considered to be a suitable wife for the oldest son of the wealthy Zorawskis. Many years later, when Maria had became famous and a statue of her was erected in Warsaw, Kazimierz could be seen gazing, deep in thought, at her face.

At last, Bronya finished her studies in Paris and married a Polish doctor, Kazimierz Dluski. She wrote to Maria, asking her to stay with them in Paris while she attended the university.

Maria was scared about leaving Poland and her father. She was still timid and shy and she took a long time to make up her mind. But finally she packed her bags, took one long look at Warsaw and climbed into the train.

Goodbye Poland, goodbye Kazimierz Zorawski. Hello Paris, several years of poverty and a lifetime of hard work.

Maria and Bronya planned to live in Paris.

Paris at last!

Maria arrived in Paris in 1891. She was twenty-four. She came to be known as Marie, the French version of her name. The atmosphere in this sophisticated European city was very different from Warsaw. In Paris new ideas on all subjects were encouraged. Paris was free. Warsaw was under Russian rule. Maria had grown up with an understanding of hardship and revolution. She was shocked by the freedom of young French people.

Marie had to study in bed to keep warm.

Like many students in those days, she had barely enough food and could keep warm only by staying in bed and piling coats over her thin blankets. It was a hard life but it didn't stop her from getting top marks in her physics exams. She was a stubborn and determined girl and she wasn't going to be defeated.

After the exams she returned to Warsaw before deciding to go back to Paris and take a degree in mathematics too.

Luckily, she was awarded a scholarship. This would allow her to study for another year.

By 1894, three years after she arrived in Paris speaking very little French, Marie had completed two degrees and done very well in her exams. She now decided that she would devote her life to science.

Meanwhile she had become an attractive young woman. During her years as a starving student, she had lost weight and become paler in the face. Her eyes were beautiful and rather sad. She was shy, simply dressed, quiet and composed.

At this point she met and fell in love with her future husband, another hard-working scientist called Pierre Curie.

9

Pierre and Marie met in Paris, the sophisticated city where she now lived.

Marriage to Pierre

Pierre Curie, seven years older than Marie, was a very bright physicist, and like her he was very shy. In 1895 they married.

Bronya's mother-in-law wanted Marie to wear a white wedding dress, and offered to buy it for her. But Marie refused because she thought it was a waste of money. She chose a plain dress that she could wear to work afterward. The couple were married at a simple registry office ceremony.

For their honeymoon, Marie and Pierre set off on a bicycle tour of France. Bicycles had only recently become popular, and they brought a great sense of freedom and independence, especially for women.

Although he enjoyed the fresh air and the holiday very much, Pierre hated being away from his work. Marie wrote that every now and then he would stop and say, "It seems to me a very long time since we have accomplished anything." Even so, in future years they spent most of their vacations cycling around different areas of France and Marie remembered them as very happy times.

The Curies enjoyed a honeymoon spent touring France on bicycles. They both loved being out in the countryside.

The working mother

When they returned from their honeymoon, Marie and Pierre began to work very hard. Pierre taught at the School of Physics and Chemistry and Marie worked with him but on separate research. She started to publish papers on her work.

In 1897, their first child, Irène, was born. It was unusual in those days for women to work after they had had a baby, but Marie was determined to go on with her scientific research. She found a baby sitter for Irène and carried on. Even in the easy-going atmosphere of Paris, many people found this very strange

Marie continued her research, but still had plenty of time for her daughter Irène.

and said she was neglecting her child. In fact she was a very loving mother and was very close to her two daughters all her life.

Marie decided to study for a further degree to become a Doctor of Science. That meant she had to discover something new about a subject and then write up a report. All she had to do was decide what to discover!

In 1895, a Bavarian called

Wilhelm Röntgen had made a discovery of great importance to medicine – X-rays. He called them X-rays because X is a scientist's usual symbol for something that is not known or understood. Röntgen had discovered these rays quite by accident. Only a few days after Röntgen made his report, X-rays were used to locate a bullet embedded in a man's leg. Scientists everywhere became very excited by this new discovery.

Then in 1897 a French scientist, Henri Becquerel, found that a substance called uranium gave off rays that were very like X-rays. But there was much work to be done to find out more about uranium.

Marie decided that she would study uranium rays for her doctorate. She was offered a small, dark and damp laboratory at the School of Physics and Chemistry. She had very little equipment and no money. It was in these difficult circumstances that timid little Marie was to make an important scientific discovery that would bring her recognition all over the world and save thousands of lives.

Marie discovers radium

Working every day in the freezing cold laboratory was no fun, and finding out about uranium was a very slow business, but Marie stuck to her work.

An element is a substance that exists in a pure state and cannot be broken down into other substances. Marie started by testing every known element to see which caused air to conduct electricity and give off rays similar to those discovered by Becquerel. She described these rays as radioactive, the first time the word had been used. Marie found that there were only two such elements: thorium

Marie tested every known element.

and uranium.

Then she made another important discovery involving a substance called pitchblende, a mineral containing uranium. She saw that pitchblende was more radioactive than pure uranium, so it must contain another element that no one had yet discovered.

Pierre and Marie decided to work together to find this new element, which they called radium. In 1898 Marie published an article on her research so far and then set to work on the pitchblende.

For their experiments, the Curies needed a huge amount of pitchblende and soon it was being delivered at the door of the little laboratory in tons. It looked like piles of soil. From this heap of dirt the Curies had to isolate all the elements contained in it. What was left would be the unknown element, radium.

The work turned out to be even harder than the Curies imagined, because pitchblende contained only the tiniest amount of radium. It was therefore very

difficult to extract. Marie had to stir huge pots of it for hours at a time.

The months turned into years as Pierre and Marie worked their way through the tons of pitchblende, purifying it and extracting more and more of the known elements.

Then one evening in 1902 as they sat at home, Marie suddenly felt she must go back to the laboratory to check on her experiments of the afternoon. As she and Pierre opened the door of their little shed they saw in the darkness a faint but very definite blue glow. It was a tiny speck of pure radium!

To find the element radium, Marie had to stir huge pots of pitchblende for hours.

The importance of radium

While Pierre and Marie worked with their radioactive materials, they began to feel ill. Pierre suffered from strange pains in his limbs, and both he and Marie were very easily tired and often came down with colds and other annoying illnesses. Their fingers were cracked too from contact with the elements they handled, and both of them suffered from blisters and sores on their hands which would not heal.

We now know more about radiation sickness. It is hardly surprising that they became ill when they were working with

Marie's laboratory equipment. Some of it was too radioactive to be touched for sometime after all her experiments with radium.

radioactive substances all day long. Three of the Curies' notebooks were considered too dangerous to handle because of radioactivity seventy-five years after they had been written.

Despite their illnesses, they worked on. They wrote many reports on radium which were read by doctors and scientists all over the world. Their work led to many exciting discoveries. Although it looked as if radium could cause illness in people who worked with it, it could also be used to cure diseases. Scientists discovered that it could be used to treat patients with cancer, by directing radiation onto the unhealthy cells to destroy their growth.

Suddenly the Curies were famous. They received letters from all kinds of people asking how they had separated radium from pitchblende. At this point they could have become very rich. They could have patented their find, which meant that anyone wanting to know the secret of radium would have to pay for the information. But, even though

The Curies' discovery of radium helped to create a new treatment for cancer.

they badly needed money for a new laboratory, Pierre and Marie would not take money for something they now knew could save lives.

Marie Curie wrote her long report, or thesis, on radium, and in 1903, when she was 36 years old, she was awarded the degree of Doctor of Science. For the ceremony she actually bought a new dress – again, dark and very simple. She stood up in a huge room full of eminent scientists and explained her findings. She and Pierre were world famous.

A great honor

Everyone now wanted to meet the couple who had discovered radium. In June 1903 they were invited to London to talk at the Royal Institution where scientists and ordinary people alike could go to hear about interesting new discoveries.

A large audience came to the Royal Institution to hear the Curies talk. There were parties and banquets too where Marie, dressed in plain clothes as usual, found herself surrounded by glamorous women wearing jewels and very expensive dresses.

Later that year they received a very special prize. A telegram arrived at their home telling the Curies that they had been awarded the Nobel Prize in physics which was to be shared with their friend, Henri Becquerel. With the prize came money. Neither Pierre nor Marie felt up to making the journey or going through the ceremony. Henri Becquerel brought their gold medals with him back to France.

Marie was not interested in fashion. She wore plain old dresses to parties.

But 1903 was not all fame and fortune. Both Marie and Pierre were becoming more ill with the effects of radiation, and late in 1903 Marie became pregnant. Unfortunately, the baby died soon after it was born.

The Nobel Prize money was very useful to Pierre and Marie. It meant they could buy new equipment and work even harder. Pierre was made a professor at the Sorbonne.

But now there were annoying

A medal commemorating Marie's and Pierre's discovery of radium. Suddenly, they had become very famous.

interruptions from journalists who wanted to write about them in newspapers, and from companies and individuals asking them to talk about their work all over the world. They hated the public life and longed to get back to work together quietly. It was a very difficult time. Marie became pregnant again and after a difficult time gave birth to Eve, her second daughter, who later wrote her mother's life story. 1904

Tragedy and triumph

It was lunchtime on April 19, 1906 and it was raining. Pierre and a group of his physicist friends sat in a hotel on the Left Bank of Paris discussing university business. Marie was at home giving the children their lunch. It was clear to all his friends that Pierre was ill and very frail.

Pierre left the meeting to go and see his publishers. The offices were closed and he turned to cross the road.

As he did so he was hit by the wheel of a large, horse-drawn

Pierre was hit by a horse-drawn cart and died instantly.

cart and killed instantly. The driver was in tears. He said of Pierre, "He was walking quickly, his umbrella was up in his hand and he literally threw himself on my left-side horse." Pierre's body was taken to his home and Marie was told the news. She was extremely upset. She and Pierre had lived and worked together. He was her constant companion. How could she go on without him?

Scientists everywhere were shocked too. Although it was Marie who had first found that radium must exist, Pierre had given up his own work on crystals to help her separate pure radium from pitchblende.

The funeral was attended by many scientists and Marie received hundreds of letters from people who sympathized with her.

Although Marie was deeply sad, she was determined to go on working. Soon after the accident the Sorbonne offered her Pierre's job as head of the Physics department and Marie Curie became a professor, the first woman in France to receive that honor. She was offered a good salary and facilities for research.

Marie became the first woman professor in France. She lectured at the Sorbonne University in Paris.

She took the job but wanted to be accepted for her own work, not because of her husband.

This was to be the case. Her first lecture as Professor was very well attended and everyone clapped very loudly at the end. One person wrote of the occasion in a newspaper, claiming "the celebration of a victory for feminism. If a woman is allowed to teach advanced studies to both sexes, where afterwards will be the pretended superiority of man . . .?"

21

Difficult times

1911 was an awful year for Marie Curie. She became very fond of fellow scientist Paul Langevin. Because he was married with four children, some people felt it was wrong for her to be friendly with him. The newspapers of the day exaggerated the story and helped to make her life miserable.

She received hundreds of hate letters through the mail and became ill with worry and very depressed, even considering suicide. It was terrible to have made a home in a foreign city, become one of its most famous citizens ever and then be rejected by the very people who had cheered her work only a few years before.

In 1910 Marie Curie had published another long paper on radioactivity and this time it was all her own work. She was given a second Nobel Prize, and became the only person ever to receive this award twice. Some scientists

Cruel People sent Marie hate letters, because she had become very fond of a married man. She felt sad and lonely.

did not believe she deserved it because there were many other people who had made important discoveries too. Others thought she had been given it to make up for the sad time she was having in her personal life.

This time she went to Stockholm to receive the prize, but it exhausted her. She became ill and had to go to a nursing home to recover.

At this point she became interested in the Suffragette Movement in England. She went to stay with Hertha Ayrton, who was campaigning to have three suffragettes released from prison. Mrs. Ayrton was very good at keeping newspaper men and

Marie ran the new Radium Institute.

detectives away from Marie. Marie soon recovered enough strength to go back to Paris and start work again.

It had been a terrible year, but once again Marie Curie returned to her laboratory. And now the Sorbonne decided to build a special Radium Institute and put her in charge. She was to have her own place of work and it was to be built in a road renamed rue Pierre Curie. Marie Curie was excited and took a special interest in the building. It was finished on July 31, 1914. In many ways it was bad timing because only a few days later World War I began and all the men working in her laboratory had to go and fight.

Marie continued to work despite her many problems.

23

War work

Marie Curie, the Polish girl who loved her country fiercely, now felt she had become French. She decided to serve in the war as best she could.

First she made sure her children were well cared for and safely out of Paris. Her next thought was for her precious gram of radium that she had given to the university. It would be terrible if it was lost in a bombing raid.

Many people were panicking and leaving Paris for the country. Marie jumped on an overcrowded train and took the radium to Bordeaux where she put it in the vaults of a bank. She then headed back to Paris to do something useful.

She toured the city on buses, horse-drawn cabs and automobiles, which she borrowed and called on rich people to ask them for money. She wanted to buy cars and vans that she could fit up with X-ray equipment to help wounded soldiers. She raised the money easily. Then she went to companies who made scientific

instruments and asked for their help too.

During the war Marie Curie, with the help of her older daughter, Irène, provided more than 200 cars holding X-ray equipment. Her friends also set up centers near the battlefields so that X-ray pictures could be taken of the soldiers' wounds right on the spot.

X-rays are special photographs that show up bullets, damaged bones and other wounds inside the body. In the case of soldiers, the X-rays told doctors right away exactly what was wrong so that they could act quickly and save lives.

Soon, Marie Curie decided that Irène could be left in charge at the front while Marie went back to the Radium Institute to teach young girls how to use X-ray equipment. Irène was not yet eighteen years old.

Marie Curie hated the war. So many young soldiers were killed or badly injured. But her hard work meant that in just one year of the war her team of helpers X-rayed more than 1,100,000 men.

Irène and Marie X-rayed many wounded soldiers during the war.

A visit to the White House

Ever since she had first received the Nobel Prize, reporters had wanted to interview Marie Curie. She was shy and usually refused. Then after the war had ended, an American reporter, named Marie Meloney, tried so hard to see her that Marie Curie decided she would give her an interview. The two women became firm friends.

By this time some doctors had cured patients of cancer with radium treatment. Mrs. Meloney found out that there was only one gram of radium in the whole of France. She was determined that that should change.

When she went back to the United States she began to raise the money – $100,000 – to buy another gram of radium for

The White House, where Marie was welcomed by President Harding.

The President presented Marie with a key to a casket of much-needed radium.

Marie Curie's Radium Institute in Paris. She traveled around America with some friends, talking to people, and asking for money. She raised the money and asked Marie to come to America to receive the radium. Marie was reluctant, but eventually she agreed and brought with her Irène and her younger daughter Eve.

She received a big welcome in America. People cheered her and threw parties in her honor. Then Marie went to the White House where President Harding presented her with a gold key that would open the casket of radium.

The people of France felt ashamed that the Americans should be so generous to Marie Curie when they had done so little to help her. The troubles of 1911 were forgotten and one newspaper editor now called her "the greatest woman in France."

Marie was grateful to Mrs. Meloney for all her help and wanted to pay her back. She made sure that she was rewarded with the *Légion d'Honneur* (Legion of Honor), a special award that is given to only a few people.

Hard work rewarded

Meanwhile Marie Curie had been slowly going blind. She had heard that people who worked with radium had become ill and died, although she did not want to believe that the precious radium was to blame. Apart from her eye trouble and her past illnesses, she was still strong and working hard.

She traveled all over the world giving lectures. Scientists from Italy, Holland, England, Spain, Czechoslovakia and Brussels all asked her to come and talk to them. Even in China, in the temple of Confucius at Taiyuanfu, there was a portrait of Madame Marie Curie. She was given many more medals and prizes and became an honorary member of more than eighty scientific societies.

Her one wish now was for Warsaw, her home city, to have a Radium Institute. She and Bronya collected money to build the Institute, and Bronya spent much time helping the architects and builders design the building. At last, in 1925, Marie's dream came true. Although she was almost blind, she traveled to Warsaw. The President of Poland laid the first stone of the building and Marie Curie laid the second.

Marie worked on despite the illness she suffered from exposure to radioactivity.

She received a second gram of radium from the United States and this she gave to the Radium Institute of Warsaw.

When she was 66 years old she suddenly became ill with a blood disease caused by close contact with radioactive substances over many years. It was the same disease that had made Pierre feel so weak.

Her last words, as she lay dying in a nursing home, were "I want to be left in peace." She died in 1934, at the age of 66.

Her friends tried to keep the newspaper reporters from coming to the private family funeral, so that her last wish would be granted. But Marie Curie was too famous. They climbed the cemetery walls to get a last look at France's best-known scientist.

Marie Curie was a tough and determined woman, dedicated to working for others. She was not interested in fame for herself and only accepted honors because in this way radium became known throughout the world and could be used to cure terrible diseases. Her work was her gift to the world and she gave it freely and willingly.

Marie Curie worked with dedication throughout her life, for the advancement of science and for the good of the world.

29

Important dates

1867	Maria Sklodowska (later Marie Curie) born in Warsaw (November 7).
1876	Sofia, Maria's oldest sister, dies of tuberculosis.
1878	Maria's mother dies of the same disease.
1882	Maria wins a gold medal at school and is sent to the country for a year.
1885	Maria takes her first job as a governess. A failure.
1886	Maria goes to the Zorawski family as a governess. She enjoys herself and stays for over three years. She becomes interested in science, particularly physics and mathematics.
1891	Maria arrives in Paris to study at the Sorbonne University.
1893	Maria takes top place in her physics exam.
1894	She comes second in her mathematics exam.
1895	Maria marries Pierre Curie.
1897	Their first child, Irène, born (September 12).
1898	Marie and Pierre work together to try to discover radium.
1902	The couple succeed in purifying a speck of radium.
1903	Marie becomes a Doctor of Science with a report on radium and the Curies win the Nobel Prize for Physics along with their friend, Henri Becquerel.
1904	Second daughter, Eve, is born (December 6).
1906	Pierre is killed in a road accident (April 19). Marie takes his job as Head of the Physics Department at the Sorbonne.
1910	Marie publishes *Treatise on Radioactivity*.
1911	Marie wins the Nobel Prize for the second time.
1914	Radium Institute of Paris finished. Marie is in charge.
1914–18	During the war Marie organizes a team of people to drive X-ray vans to the battlefields so that wounded soldiers can be treated properly.
1921	Marie makes a tour of the United States, helped by her journalist friend, Marie Meloney. She receives a gram of radium from President Harding at the White House.
1925	Radium Institute of Warsaw is finished. Marie and her sister Bronya had helped raise the money to build it.
1934	(July 6). Death of Marie Curie.

Glossary

Element A pure substance that cannot be broken down into other substances. All known things are made up of elements.

Mineral A substance, made by nature, that was never animal or vegetable. Some minerals are made up of a single element, but most are compounds, i.e. made up of more than one substance.

Pitchblende A soft rock that contains uranium and radium.

Radiation sickness An illness suffered by people who come into contact with radioactive substances.

Radioactive Giving off dangerously powerful rays as a result of changes in the nuclei of atoms. The rays can cause burns and sickness. Uranium is a radioactive substance.

Radiotherapy A treatment for cancer using radium.

Radium The radioactive element discovered by Marie and Pierre Curie. Radium is dangerous to work with but is used in cancer treatment, too.

Thorium Another element giving off radioactive rays.

Uranium A radioactive element.

X-rays Powerful rays, discovered by the scientist Röntgen. X-rays can pass through most things except metal and bone. They are used to take photographs of the inside of the body.

Books to read

Brandt, Keith. *Marie Curie: Brave Scientist*. Troll Associates, 1983.

Farr, Naunerle. *Madame Curie – Albert Einstein*. Pendulum Press, 1979.

Greene, Carol. *Marie Curie: Pioneer Physicist*. Children's Press, 1984.

Henbest, Nigel and Heather Couper. *Physics*. Franklin Watts, 1983.

Keller, Mollie. *Marie Curie*. Franklin Watts, 1982.

Mandell, Muriel. *Physics Experiments for Children*. Dover, 1968.

Young, Marvin and Lee Garfield. *Science is Inquiring*. Modern Curriculum Press, 1981.

Picture credits

BBC Hulton Picture Library 23 (below), 28, 29; Mary Evans Picture Library 10, 17, 21; The Mansell Collection 14, 23 (above); Ann Ronan Picture Library 19. Cover artwork by Richard Hook.

Index